Florence

Mysterious

TIT-BITS 2

Rev Gerogina Mensah-Brown

Florence - Mysterious Tit-Bits 2

Rev Georgina Mensah-Brown

Paperback Edition First Publishing in Great Britain in 2015 by aSys Publishing

eBook Edition First Publishing in Great Britain in 2014 by aSys Publishing

Copyright © Georgina Mensah-Brown

All rights reserved.

No part of this document may be reproduced or transmitted in any form or by any means, electronic, mechanical, photocopying, recording, or otherwise, without prior written permission of the Author.

ISBN: 978-1-910757-18-5

aSys Publishing

http://www.asys-publishing.co.uk

Dedication

Dedicated to Mr Stephen Brown my husband, To Mr and Mrs Florence Ampah - Agyekum, a member of the Westminster Central Hall Methodist church, London. United Kingdom. A member of the church team of florists. Also a steward of the Ghana Methodist Fellowship. (GMF) To Eva Effie Dacosta, a dedicated sister in the service of the Lord. To Sister Ewuradwoa Ferguson and the stewards of Walworth Methodist church. To sister Florence Acquah Taylor a member of the Archway Methodist Church and a senior steward of the Ghanaian Methodist Fellowship UK 2008-2013. To Mr Kodwo Arko (my spiritual next door neighbour). To sister Eva De Graft, A circuit steward. To all past Summa presidents. Grace Acheampong, Nana Ama Brahene, Eve and Janet. To Christiana Mensah, the Church choir and all the choristers of Walworth Methodist Church. Clubland. London UK. To Mr Olu Senior and Hilton Olu Junior, Mr Ernest Owen, past pastoral secretary. Rev Eric Mustapha, the residential minister of the Walworth Methodist Church, Club land. UK. (2001-2014). To all members of the Walworth Methodist church. To the Walworth Ghana Methodist Fellowship, (GMF) UK. Sister Edna Opata and Sister Susanna Anobil, past presidents, Women's; fellowship. Sisters, Mercy, Aggie, Doris and Grace, Lydia and co, To Mr and Mrs Charway, to Mr and Mrs Banwell. To Mrs Osiyeme Mr and Mrs Caroline Ogunsola.

To the Sierra Leone Fellowship Walworth, Nigeria Fellowship, The Caribbeans, Gambians and Zimbabwean Fellowships of the Walworth Methodist church UK. To the Wednesday Fellowship, Mr Olu, Mr Ofori Mensah, Mr David Pandah

Noah, Tricia Hemans, Mr Kwame and Joycelyn, Sister Olu Akiyeme. To the Wonders of Walworth.

To Mr and Mrs Hannah Quainoo, Ghana. To Seth and Nancy Okine Accra Ghana, My In-law Mrs Lydia Okine. To sister Lovia and her family. To Sister Mary Quainoo, To the Calvary Methodist Church Enchi. Ghana.

Finally to the Methodist Church Ghana, and all Christians.

Appreciation

Thanks to my husband Stephen, for his support and
encouragement. To God be the glory,
great things he has done.

Preface

We live in a world of a thousands of unknowns. The search for knowledge has been on for ages, to dig into the mystery of life, yet the unknown remains unknown. We have tried with our imaginations, historical facts, scientific evidence and archaeological discoveries, and the Bible, to find about things beyond our imaginations and thinking, but sometimes we remain shut up in the midst of numerous unanswered mysteries surrounding our humanity and places of dwelling. Those who have gone ahead of us had many things to tell about life, which they struggled to know and understand. After comparing all their knowledge and discoveries to our own modern and advanced searches, we are still left with many unknown facts about life, which we may believe, but cannot tell. Even if Methuselah, the oldest man on earth was still living, he equally, may not have had all the answers to our questions, because he was also caught up in the unknown. The spiritual cloud of witnesses of the dead, may now have knowledge of the unknown because of their changed realm, but they are not able to give information about them, because they have not been given the power to do so. They may be hovering around us with answers to the mysterious, but they are hidden from our sight, and utterance except with the eye of faith.

We may not know we cannot tell, is a book written basically within the African concept of human life, which sometimes poses a challenge to the Christian faith. It brings to mind the limitation of our being, as humans and what we may never ever know, because they have not been given to us, but we know one day we shall know as they are known.

Chapter 1
AFTER LIFE

"The secret things belong to the Lord our God, but the things that are revealed, belong to us, and our children forever." Deuteronomy 29:29.

This bible passage clearly answers the question of things which are being hidden from human beings and we may not find answers because they are not to be revealed. Christian theology and experience brings to knowledge about human questions, however, certain things happening around our daily living prompts us to question those things which have no answers for us now. Many people know that there is life after death. Christians believe in heaven and hell in the afterlife. Traditionalist believes in death as a life of living with ancestors and staying with them in the land of the death. Other people also believe in both as well. The belief in the powers of the dead to act is very rare in some traditions.

Some friends and family members of the dead do speak to the dead and some extend their greetings to their dead relatives as the body is laid in state, or being carried to the cemetery for burial. Some also weep as they follow the coffin and send messages via the dead relative saying, "Good bye our love. When you see my mother, extend my greetings to her. Tell uncle Kofi that we greet him." These are moving moments when some other dead relatives are remembered as they weep for those who have died. People weep for older dead relatives as well as the newly dead. Thus all weeping at funerals, may not be related to the newly dead per se, but people remember their love ones who have equally passed away.

Speaking and extending greetings to the long dead relatives, whilst others speak to the dead body who is laid in state, means the dead person hears all what they are being told. It could be mysterious but we may not know, we cannot tell, whether the dead do actually listen, because some actually do respond to what they are told in diverse ways.

In the oden days, a dead relative could be given a knife to kill those who caused their death if the family were hit by the sudden or a premature death of that person. These happen when a young and a promising member of the person dies. Some actually take revenge on their culprits who caused their deaths. Thus people bath concoctions against the spirit of the death whilst some also put concoctions on graves to restrict the spirit of the dead. Fetish priests gives such concoctions or rituals to prevent the ghost from coming out from their graves to attack culprits who caused their death.

We may not know we cannot tell, but events which happen within some traditions presuppose that, the dead do listen if it is not the demonic activities of other powers at work.

A deceased woman who was laid in state was slapped in the face by a brother of out pain and grief. The man died two weeks later. The reason given was that the ghost or the spirit of the dead woman said, his brother had disgraced her for slapping her whilst she was laid in state. We may not know we cannot tell, but we believe it is because of some of these, that people give good tributes to their death, even when they are not always true. The dead see and listen. We may not know we cannot tell, because we have not died before.

In the Holy Scriptures, the Bible depicts the nature of life after death. The dead are kept until the day of judgement. The righteous will be raised to be with God the Father, in the new heaven and earth to come. This is what Christian's who are alive have not seen, but believe.

John 5:28-29

Marvel not at this: for the hour is coming, in which all that are in the grave shall hear his voice, and they shall come forth. They that have done good, unto the resurrection of life; and they that have done evil, unto the resurrection of damnation."(King James. Reference edition)

John 14:1-3, "Let not your hearts be troubled, you believe in God, believe also in me, in my Father's house there are many mansions, if it were not so I would have told you that I go to prepare a place for you. And when I go and prepare a place for you, I will come again and take you unto myself, that where I am, there you may be also."

Revelation chapter 21:3-4 "And I heard a loud voice saying, "now the dwelling of God is with men, and he will live with them. They will be his people and God himself will be with them and be their God. He will wipe every tear from their eyes. There will be no more death, no more mourning or crying or pain, for the old order of things have passed away." (NIV).

Revelation 21:1 "And I saw a new heaven and a new earth. The first heaven and the first earth had passed away and there was no longer any sea."

Revelation 20:10 "And the devil who had deceived them was thrown was thrown into the lake of fire and sulphur where the beast and the false prophets were, and they will be tormented day and night for ever and ever. And if anyone's name was not found written in the book of life, He was thrown into the lake of fire." (15)

This is the reality of the afterlife for the created human beings on earth, who have been created in the image of God and the likeness of God. God himself shall dwell with them and be their God. This may not affect human beings, who believe God did not create them. Whether they believe there was creation at all. For people whom God did not create, they may have their own end, with whoever created them or wherever they surfaced into the world. For those whom God created in his own image, this is what awaits for them as humans.

Genesis 1: 26-27 "Then God said, 'Let us make man in our image, after our likeness. And let them have dominion over the fish of the sea, the birds of the heavens and over the livestock and over every creeping thing that creeps on the earth'. So God created man in his own image, in the image of God he created him. Male and female he created them."

Genesis 2:7 "And the Lord God created human being in his own image and after his own likeness, and breath into his nostrils the breathe of life and man became a living being."

Genesis 1:31 "And the Lord God saw everything that he has made, and it was very good."

If we were created by God as human beings, then we believe we shall see the reality of what is written in the book of Revelation as has been quoted above; when we die and reach to either of them. We may not know, we cannot tell, until we get there in death, but the just who live by faith see them far away with the eyes of faith just as other faithful believers who have passed away.

"The righteous will live by faith." Romans 1:17.

If we died and there was no heaven, as some doubting Thomas may fear, we lose nothing, but when we die and there is really Heaven and we actually did nothing about our salvation whilst on earth, then there will be a problem. It is rather good and advisable for one to choose what is good, and live the life of godliness, because that is heavenly promised.

John 3:16. "For God so loved the world, that he gave his only begotten Son, that whosoever believes in him, should not perish, but have everlasting life."

Hebrews 10:26-27. "If we deliberately keep on sinning, after we have received knowledge of the truth, the sacrifice for sins is left, but only a fearful expectation of judgement and of raging fire that would consume the enemies of God. It is a dreadful thing to fall into the hands of the living God." (Verse 31)

Many then, will weep and gnash their teeth as they are turned to hell's fire. This is going to happen because if there is heaven, then there is hell. If there is no heaven, there is no hell, but the seekers of heaven believe in heaven through the coming of Jesus Christ into our world, his life and teachings as well as his and death and ascension, confirming with his words about heaven and hell. The story of Lazarus and the rich man by Jesus shows that, one of the two men, who was called by name Lazarus, went to a place of bliss, or rest and enjoyment whilst the other went to the place of torment and weeping. In hades or the land of the dead, the rich man had wanted to send a message to his brothers who were alive on the earth, to confirm the reality of hell, and the reality of heaven, but he was not allowed.

> *Verse 22 "The poor man died and was carried by the angels to Abraham's side. The rich man also died and was buried. And in Hades, being in torment, he lifted up his eyes and saw Abraham far off and Lazarus by his side. And he cried out, father Abraham, have mercy on me and send Lazarus that he may dip the tip of his finger in water and cool my tongue. For I am tormented in this flame ..."*
>
> *"And he said, then I beg you father, to send to my father's house, for I have five brothers, so that they may warn them, lest they also come into this place of torment."*

Sometimes people do take things for granted until the reality comes. It became too late for the rich to try to make a change, either for himself or for his brothers with messengers. We may not know we cannot tell fate of the five brothers, but we must equally think of where to spend eternity.

> *Hebrews 2:3a. "Therefore we must pay much closer attention to what we have heard. For since the message proved to be declared by angels proved to be reliable and every transgression or disobedience received a just retribution. How can we escape if we neglect so great a salvation? It was first declared by the Lord, and it was attested by those who heard, while God also bore witness by signs and wonders and various miracles and by gifts of the Holy Spirit distributed according to his will."*

We may not know we cannot tell how our relatives and love ones or members of the church who had died, often want to tell us the reality of the truth of what they heard about the 'after world,' when they lived amongst us, but they are not allowed. We see their shadows in very short dreams, but where and what they are and going through, we may not know we cannot tell, unless we get there.

Jesus says, "I am the way, the truth and the life. No one comes to the Father except through me." John 14: 6.

Paul says, "Work out your own salvation with fear and trembling " Philippians 2:12b

Such passages, and many more from the Bible, are for the direction of people on the earth, who are journeying into the next world of the unknown, but the choice is for people to choose. The bliss of heaven or the furnace of Hell. God does not compel people to go, but will make us willing to go, if we want him to make us, because he is the way, the truth and the life, and the hereafter.

Apart from human belief in dead and afterlife, there are things which are hard to believe and they may be rare in our time, or our conclusion on them, with our modern generation. Modern civilization has thrown more light in mysteries of days of old with research. Modern enlightenment in Christianity is different from times of old, with modern historical and archival facts, as compared to early times of the Christian religion. Gone are the days when many Christians in Africa had the thought of a heavenly Jerusalem than earthly Jerusalem. This may have passed away for our generation of Christians, and the global world of today, with modern trend of travelling and pilgrimages to Jerusalem. In our daily living many mysteries surround us, which we may not know, we cannot tell, but we believe.

Chapter 2

THE MYSTERY OF DEATH

John Wesley Powell had this saying about the mystery of the unknown "We are now ready to start on our way down the Great Unknown. Our boat are chatting each other, and they are tossed by the fretful river... We have an unknown distance yet to run. An unknown river yet to explore. What falls there are, we know not; what wall rise over the river, we know not."

Death is a mystery, so the elders say. Death is a non-awakening sleep, so the bidding "goodnight". 'If you do not know what death is like, then look at 'sleep' so the proverbs goes among the Akan's in Ghana. What really is death to humans? 'It is the extinction of life' and they move forward or onwards to the unknown and they would not wake up until the heavens are no more.

> *Genesis, 1:6. "Now Joseph and all his brothers died, and all that generation died". Revelation 20:11-12 "And I saw a great white throne, and him that sat on it, from whose face the heavens passed away. And I saw the dead, small and great stand before God..."*
>
> *Psalm 146 verse 3-4, "Do not put your trust in princes, in mortal man, who cannot save. When their spirits*

departs they return to the ground. On that very day, their plans come to nothing"

What would it be like if humans knew their day or date of death. If at birth, the date of death is also calculated and given through science or other medical means. What would the world be like if each one knew the day of his or her death? How many people would care to go for a calculator of heart beat, which is able to determine the number of beats one is left with and days to live? How many healthy people would have been interested for this check-up? We do not know and may not want to know either. Some would surely love, to have known their day of death or 'death dates' as to confess their wrongs before they died or did more good or worse to cause more evil before they died. The good believers would have further gone ahead to beg their victims of offence for forgiveness before they died. Some worshippers of God have sometimes been teased as clapping and praising for the heavenly, yet ran away from death when they see death approaching . The mystery of death continues with its grip of fear on all except the bold ones who faces death squarely through any means. Even in this way, they may still think quietly about the unknown before plunging themselves into it to face the reality of death, after they close their eyes in death to our world, and open their spiritual eyes in another realm to face what is awaiting them. We may not know, we cannot tell where we came from except from the dust of the ground, but we may know where we are going.

Traditions have it that those who are bold enough to buy their coffins to keep long before they die, or people for whom coffins are bought because of long illness also to keep for a long time before they die. Does death fear a coffin before it attacks its victims? Definitely not. Otherwise everyone will buy a coffin and some will even make a coffin their bed at night, and there will be a fashion of coffins in people's homes if not rather "coffin-home- cemeteries." Even with this, we may not know we cannot tell, yet we can tell of people who bought their coffins and death was delayed for a long time before surfacing. The saying that, "cowards die long before their time" can be true as the adage goes, but would being bold to buy your coffin in old age help keep you longer in life before death? This we may not, know we cannot tell, but we believe.

Death is a mystery and very hard to comprehend. When someone dies, it seems like a dream to some relatives in many cases. Is it real that the person is dead? Are we no more going to see that love one again? Is that what life is all about? Is the dead person not going to come back again? As we stand by their bedside or grave side what goes on in our heads? When the graves are being covered, with the sound of the banking of the sands and stones, do they register any message in our hearts and mind? Death is the end of it all with the person. The one who died is seen no more in this life and forever. They will never be seen. Until the heavens are no more, they will never wake from their sleep. The book of Job has many things to say about death.

> ***Job 14:11-12 "As the waters fall from the sea and the flood decay and dry up, so man lie down and rise not, till the heavens be no more they shall not awake nor be raised up from their sleep".(KJV)***

> ***Job 14:7-10. "For there is hope of a tree, if it is cut down, that it will sprout again. And that the tender branch thereof will not cease. Though the roof thereof wax old in the earth, and the stock thereof die in the ground; Yet through the scent of the water, it will bud, and bring***

forth buds like a plant. But man dies and wasted away, Yea, man gives up the ghost, and where is he?"

Job 7:9-10, "As the cloud is consumed and vanishes away, so he that goes down to the grave, shall come up no more. He shall return no more to his house, neither shall his place know him anymore."

Humanity until late, has not been able to conquer or overcome death in the form of treatment of diseases, or bring back to life after death takes place despite all the advancement in medical science and treatments, even to heart surgeries or transplant. What human beings have been able to do is to prevent or extend the time of death by the breakthrough of medication for killer diseases, which had no cure in times past and without good medication. Death still continues since the time of Abel in the book of Genesis. What we have been told in death or after death is only for our ears, since humans have not been given the divine authority over death or to visit the land of the dead and come back like a holiday visit. The lenses in our physical eyes have not been given the power to see from the other realm of spirits with a long sight not even that of the lens of the eyes of the eagle. Only the dead know where they are and what is happening in their realm of spirits.

The hymnist wrote,

> **"Lord it belongs not to my care whether I die or live. To love and serve thee is my share, and this thy grace must give,**
>
> **If live be long, I will be glad, that I may long obey, If short, yet why should I be sad, To soar to endless day?**
>
> **My knowledge of that life is small; The eye of faith is**

dim. But tis enough, that Christ knows all, And I shall be with him."

Richard Baxter(1615-91)

Augustine Toplady also wrote,

"When I draw this fleeting breath, when I close my eyes in death. When I soar to worlds unknown: See thee on thy judgement throne. Rock of ages cleft for me, Let me hide myself in thee."

Augustine Montague Toplady (1740-1778)

There are old stories of dying people coming back to life and living with people on earth for a while before someone who knew them saw them and they then vanished and were seen no more. What has science or religion done so far, to reveal such ghosts or living death so that they do not vanish, so that the living might question them about the afterlife? Or have they ceased at all? We may not know we cannot tell, but we believe living ghosts are not welcomed by the modern people of today, because many have no time for anyone in the name of ghost or whatever except the traditional believers. Moreover people are much busier with modern hectic life styles than before, so whether one is a ghost or not, it is for the living ghost to sort himself or herself out.

Jesus' Death

Jesus died and entered the spirit realm of ghost or dead people. After his death, Jesus appeared to his disciples. He allowed Thomas to touch him and feel his wounded sides.

John 20:25-28. Now Thomas, one of the twelve, called the twin, was not with them when Jesus came. So the other disciples told him, "We have seen the Lord". But he said to them, "Unless I see in his hands, the mark of the nails, and place my hands into his side, I will not believe." Eight days later, his disciples were inside again, and Thomas was with them. Although the doors were locked, Jesus came and stood among them and said, "Peace be with you". Then he said to Thomas, "Put your finger here, and see my hands". And put out your hand and place it in my side". Do not disbelieve, but believe.

No dead person or ghost has been able to reveal himself or herself to be touched and remained the same. Whenever a ghost allowed to be touched, he or she changes or vanishes. Of late we do not hear living ghost living among people. Years back, such stories existed. There was the case of a woman in a traditional area some twenty five years ago, who was claimed to have died and came back life. She might be dead again by now and this also raises another question about the dead who comes back to live to die again or 're-die'. We may not know we cannot tell but we believe. These were the days when children of such dead people were sent by their dead mother to a town or a village into a particular house and asked for a name, which the children did not know to be their living mother who was known by the villagers to be dead. The relatives sees straight away that their dead relative was somewhere and has had children and had brought them back to her relatives. Lack of knowledge has also played down on many communities of such where unclean spirits can turn many things around to confirm Satan's power and deception or anyone sending an unwanted child to be looked after. In all education and Christian enlightenment has helped to eleviate such events.

In the case of the dead woman who came back to life, she went to the chief's palace and reported herself to the chief and his elders that she was the dead, who had come back to life. Her story was that when she was a young woman she was married to a man who had another wife and her rival bewitched her through the occult and she died through child birth. That was more than twenty five years back. She reincarnated and went to another place and got married. She was said to have been violent and liked fighting people especially when the women went to fetch water and struggled for water. According to this 'reincarnated woman', her in-law was someone who was also strong in spiritism. After sometime her in-law noticed her behaviour to be unusual and in the spirit saw her not to be a real human person but a ghost. He stiffed the woman one day with a plant concoction and this debarred her from changing into her ghost state any longer. When her husband died, she had no option than to go back to her own people where she had been buried for more than thirty years ago. She showed the chief and the elders the marks on her body which was to proof she was the same person, and some of the elders did agreed that a sort of a young woman lived and died in a particular family. This happened when the chief had assembled his elders to listen to her story. Her relatives were mostly dead by that time. The chief and the elders themselves were young men at that time she was alive, but they believed her story because rumours of death's by rivals was not anything to dispute. They welcomed her back home. Sometime later, she joined a burial at the cemetery. She told those around her, pointing to the graves saying, "All these are empty tombs. No one is inside. Their spirits move away from the graves after three days of burial " Where do they go then after the three days? This is the challenge which Satan might give to the people on the earth that the dead do come back to life, but for how long? We may not know we cannot tell, but this happened.

Again to the assertion or this dead-alive woman, that the spirit of the dead leave the graves after three days, is there any clue or indication in this saying, and if it is true at all? Can we relate this to the three days Jesus spent in the grave and came back to life? Jesus had already predicted to come out from the death after three days.

> *John 2:19. "Jesus answered them, Destroy this temple, and I will raise it again in three days."*
>
> *Matthew. 12:40 "For as Jonah was three days and three nights in the belly of a huge fish, so the son of man will be three days and three nights in the heart of the earth."*
>
> *Matthew 20:17-19. "Now as Jesus was going to Jerusalem, he took the twelve disciples aside and said to them, "We are going to Jerusalem, and the son of man will be betrayed to the chief priest and the teachers of the law. They will condemn him to death and will turn him over to the gentiles to be mocked and flogged and crucified. On the third day, he will be raised to life"*
>
> *1 Corinthians 15:3, "For what I received, I pass on to you, as of first importance, that Christ died for our sins, according to the scriptures, that he was buried, and was raised on the third day according to the scriptures, and that he appeared to Peter, and then to the twelve."*

Is there any theology of the number 'three' with the death, or of the 'three days' of Jesus' body in the grave? Why three days and not two or seven days? We may not know we cannot tell, but we believe that the Hebrews have reasons for the numbers of days like three and seven or forty, and if the number three is used for the dead in the case of Jesus and for human beings when they die, but we believe the Bible talks about the Last day.

Genesis 1:13. "And there was morning and evening, The third day".

What was the nature of the body with which Jesus rose with? This story of the reincarnated woman, is some of the things Satan does, to dissuade people from believing the gospel truth with deceptive and out-twisted facts. They see it and they believe it, but is it the gospel truth? We may not know we cannot tell, but in the gospel facts, we believe.

Jesus was not a ghost. Jesus challenged Peter and the others when he appeared unto them that a ghost does not eat, but Jesus ate with them after his resurrection. This is also a clue for those who put down food for their dead to eat. Such food are for unclean spirits to operate on. Jesus eating after he rose from the dead means he was a different personal being with a heavenly body. By rising from the dead Jesus showed his followers and Christians the nature of the new body of believers when they are raised from dead. Again Jesus physically did eat.

John 21:1 "After these things, Jesus showed himself again to the disciples at the sea of Tiberius".

Verse 10 Jesus said to them, "Bring of the fish which ye have now caught, Jesus said to them, and come and dine, And none of the disciples dare ask him, Who are you? Knowing that it was the Lord."

1 Corinthians 15: 42. "So will it be with the resurrection of the dead. The body that is sown is perishable. It is raised imperishable. It is sown in dishonour, it is raised with glory, It is sown in weakness, it is raised with power. It is sown a natural body, it is raised a spiritual body. If there is a natural body, there is also a spiritual body."

In another event of Jesus's death, the earth shook, the winds blew and the curtains of the temple were torn into two. Nature was sending the message. "He is the son of God, whom you have killed." A centurion replied after the earthquake.

> ***"Truly, he was the son of God" Matthew 27:54 "Now when the centurion, and they that were with him, watching Jesus, saw the earthquake, and those thing that were done, they feared greatly, saying, truly this was the Son of God."***

Was the earthquake a spiritual communication in the spirit realm announcing the appalling killing of Christ? Or Jesus using the earthquake to communicate freedom from the Law and liberation of women to approach God? In the case of the killing of the innocent Abel, the earth or the ground opened its mouth and swallowed the blood of Abel, but in the case of the innocent blood of Jesus the Christ, the earth quaked, or cried loud to indicate an Innocent's blood has been shed.

In many traditions there is the belief that the death of good and holy people may cause a sign in the sky. The same may apply to bad and evil people for nature to tell. We may not know we cannot tell. In many traditional places, the death of great people may cause gloomy clouds over the skies in their location or part of the country if the person is linked to the people as a whole, like presidents and heads of countries. Premature deaths likewise causes signs in the sky in many traditional places for people to know that someone has given up the spirit prematurely through the evil deeds of others, especially with a good person whose death was caused by other non-natural effects.

Traditionally, what is the meaning of the falling rain sometimes, when people die? There are many times when on the day that an important person died, the rain falls. Sometimes the rains came down with strong winds and thunder on the very day the person died. This may precede the announcement of the death of the dead person or after people hear of the person's death. Many people might not have taken that into consideration, but people in many traditional areas do witness things of that sort. Many have observed for some time that the rains really do fall when people die under certain strange circumstances or suddenly in tragic deaths. The rain is seen as the dissatisfaction of the dead person. Many are witnesses in many traditional areas when certain deaths occurred. On the day the dead body was brought into the house from the mortuary or on the day the body is to be laid in state, the clouds suddenly gather and it begins to drizzle or the rain falls. When this happens, a relative will stand in the middle of the house or compound and mention the name of the deceased and tell the deceased not to squeeze his or her face, but smile to show appreciation, because sympathisers and mourners are coming to their funeral. This makes the corpse to change their countenance thereafter, meaning that the one who is dead is being visited by people so the one should smile or clear their faces. Traditionally, the falling rain might mean that, the dead person is crying or weeping, and weeping in the realm of the dead, shows with rainfalls in the land of the living. Again, the body is seen to be weeping as well when tears begin to drop from the eyes if not icing tears because of the morgue where the bodies are kept. Clearing the face or smiling, will make the rain or the drizzling stop. At times, the rain falls heavily to ruin the funeral and where the funeral is on a compound, all the canopies and benches are made uncomfortable for visiting mourners. This might not necessarily happen during rainy seasons. The belief is that the deceased was crying or angry or was not happy with his or her death or even wanted to give a sign of his or her condition as being killed spiritually by someone through the occult. On the other hand if the dead do cry thus, then what is the impression of the decease body crying in the state of death? Will be tears of joy of seeing angels descending from Heaven to come for them, or tears of anguish in seeing hell's fire before them, if not ordinary ice melting down from their eyes. We may know but, cannot tell but we believe the funeral undertakers can answer best.

This experience does occur in many traditions and has been notified by some natives, and hence the belief in them. A man was burnt alive in one of the rivalry wars between two towns. The burning of the man took place in the early hours of the evening. During the night, the rain fell with a little thunder. In the morning someone, said she saw the deceased in a dream weeping around his house. Was this around the same time the rain was falling in the night? Was this dream a reality to show the position of the dead man or only a dream? We may not know we cannot tell. In another incident, a promising pregnant lady died unexpectedly and when the body was being conveyed to the mortuary, which was many miles away to the city, the rain began to fall after they had set off and it fell throughout the whole of the journey into the whole of the night. The rain fell through all the towns the corpse had to pass through. If it was an ordinary rainfall, it could have been at the town of departure and stopped, but not inter-town and villages rainfall to a long distance, which was very unusual. This sometimes does happen but was it a coincidental rainfall or dead reality? We may not know we cannot tell, but we have meteorological proofs. The weather man can testify about such rainfalls.

Two children met their untimely death. Before their burial, the rains had not fallen for a while. On the day of their burial, the rains came down, and the rain fell across the whole of the city. It did not fall like the normal fall of rain. It poured down heavily once then stopped. After some time it poured heavily again then stopped until the burial service and committal were over. There are many instances of such rains with unexpected and painful deaths but we may not read into them that they could be a message. We may not know, we cannot tell, but we believe modern advanced science will cover them up with scientific weather reports yet there are things which are above the imagination of human beings, though scientifically they could be explained or proved, but that may not nullify the fact that such things do not exist. We continue to live in a world where we cannot fully understand the mystery of the spiritual realm.

Some people are also spiritually scientific. There are people who can conjure the rain to fall. There was a mystic man who lived in a traditional area. He was known to make the rain to fall. Any time there was a concert in the town; the organizers had to go and see him and give him money or in other way pay for the weather. It might have been weather 'rate' to be paid. They had to pay the weatherman because in the first place the compound for the concert was an open place which will make people wet when the rains did fall. Secondly many people would not attend because some had to walk from the neighbouring villages to watch the concert. One concert party challenged the assertion and came to the town without going to see the occult weather man. The sky was bright the whole day into the mid-afternoon. From 4.00 pm, the clouds had started gathering. By 5.30pm, a little wind had blown with a little drizzling to announce the rain was about to fall heavily. Quickly the organisers of the concert went to see the 'weather man' and paid for a bright weather. The rain did not come and the concert went on. This man through his occult had relations with powers to cause the rain to fall, and that was someone having supernatural relations with the sky, a human being responsible for spiritual beings of the other side of our human world, to cause the clouds to fall the rain. People who go to space, or astronauts are not able to bring the rain down, despite all the fire they shoot into the skies when they take off. They have not caused any elements in the sky to fall on people. 'Apollo Eleven,' an eye disease which was named after Apollo was thought to have shaken sky particles to fall into people's eyes in Africa, when the people started going to space, but not rain, even if the assertion was true after, considering all the later space flights? We may not know we cannot tell, but we believe there is a stone from the skies which we are waiting to hit our heads, but who will be hit can be a mystery. We may not know we cannot tell, but we will agree with scientists that, there is going to be a hit from the skies. We are mysterious in life and mysterious in death.

Chapter 3

'AND WE FLY AWAY'

The psalmist says, ***"The length of our days are seventy years if we have the strength they expand to eighty, yet their span is but trouble and sorrow, for they quickly pass and we fly away". Psalm 90:10. (ESV)*** Mourners at graveside, might witness "the flying of white doves" by those who bring them to indicate the flying away of the soul of the relative who is being buried. As the dove flies away into the skies, in the same way the spirit of the dead is believed to fly away unto the unknown. This had been a traditional belief which we may not know we cannot tell, whether at death our spirits really turn into birds or we fly away like birds. In the very olden days, the sudden appearance of a white bird after the death of a relative was sometimes seen as the soul or spirit of the dead person. This was especially the belief of school children in many traditional areas. In the classroom, whenever all of a sudden, a strange or stranded bird flew inside the classroom, no one touched the bird, because psychologically they believed the bird to be the spirit of the dead. Sometimes these birds enter at a time the children are quiet or with less talking. When the teacher was teaching and a bird entered the classroom, the children took no notice of it as to run after it or catch it. Psychologically, the children silently suspected such bird to be the spirit of a dead one or a ghost. Maybe the ghost is visiting a child. No one chases the bird out from the classroom but allow the bird to hover around and fly away. In the same way when the children are talking and all of a sudden they all stop talking and the class becomes silent, one pupil will say, 'a ghost has entered here.' Indicating the reason why they all suddenly stopped talking at the same time. That was the belief of many traditional communities about the appearance of white doves in unusual circumstances.

The ship Costa Concordia, an Italian Cruise ship that partially sank when it ran aground at Isola del Giglio, Tuscany, on 13th January 2012, claimed the loss of thirty-two lives. (London Evening Standard 14TH January) As the search for survivals continued into the third day, those who watched the ship may have seen some white birds, which were flying or hovering above the ship as the searchers were looking for survivals. This would have reminded some individuals who in their school days, might have believed in the old belief of school children about the spirits of the dead in the form of birds. Some might have psychologically taken notice of the birds quietly as the birds were hovering above the skies above the wrecked ship. Could they be the spirits of some of the people who had died less than three days or those who were yet to be found? Were the hovering of the birds above the ship, naturally a sign of birds seeing the ship or people gathering, and therefore came playing around? We may not know we cannot tell, but we believe the old traditional belief in spirits which can take the form of birds or a dove to show or makes signs to humans, but there may be no scientific or natural evidence. David use the phrase "and we fly away," meaning humans, at death fly away as the birds fly away into the skies until they are no more seen. Being true or not it would not be known until we equally fly away at death.

Psalm 90:10 "The length of our days is seventy years or eighty, if we have the strength, yet their span is but trouble and sorrow, for they quickly pass, and we fly away."

The ship wrecked Costa Concordia continued to lay in the sea months after, but no birds were seen hovering like the first three days it sunk. The birds had flown away. Whether human of dead spirit birds, they were all gone.

The spirits of the dead, are believed by some native traditions, to be hovering around their surroundings before their burial, and they go or fly away three days after burial. It could be biblically agreed, that after three days of burial, the spirits go away from the grave like Jesus, who arose out of the grave at the third day. Is there any lessons for people in third after death as if Jesus wanted to teach humanity something about death? *"And the third day he arose from the dead"* (the apostles creed)

Luke 24:46 "This is what is written: The Christ will suffer and rise from the dead on the third day."

Some people also have the belief that after death the spirit of the dead hover around for forty days and are seen no more, and hence celebration of forty days for the dead. This is again in line with Jesus ascension after forty days on earth. We may not know we cannot tell but may relate the ascension day of forty days before Jesus' ascended to heaven, to the traditional beliefs of the spirit of the dead. We may not know we cannot tell, if the forty days is for those who go to where Jesus went, and how many days for those who go their own way to the unknown.

John 14:1-3 "Do not let your hearts be troubled, Trust in God, Trust also in me. In my Father's house are many rooms if it were not so, I would have told you. I am

going there to prepare a place for you, And if I go and prepare a place for you, I will come back and take you to be with me, that you also may be where I am." (NIV)

Many churches have denounced some of these assertions of the traditional forty days for the death. Many people have no connection with these beliefs anymore and we may not know we cannot tell what happens to the spirit of the death during the forty days, but we believe there may be no period of 'waiting' like any passenger station where the dead wait to go, otherwise some might miss their transport. People prepare where they will go after life with the life they lived on earth. We may not know we cannot tell but we believe.

Chapter 4

THE DYING AND THEIR GHOSTS

A minister in a village paid a pastoral visit to a dying member, and at the end of the prayers, the man was dead. What was mysterious to this minister was that during the prayers the dying man gnashed his teeth in death. To the minister, he knew the Bible says many will gnash their teeth on the judgement day. Did this man see anything whilst drawing his fleeting breath, when he was closing his eyes in death or seeing the judgement throne of God? Was there no rock of ages which had been cleft for him to hide himself in it when he was soaring to worlds unknown? Did he see God on his judgement throne? We may not know, we cannot tell. Most dying people are out of the world before they finally close their eyes in death. Some see angels around them or beings of the spirit world. Some give the time of their departure, if they gave twelve noon, at exactly twelve o'clock noon they will die.

Children of godly parent's especially pious men and women have witnessed such deaths. Some clearly tell those around them that the hour has come and they are going. Others say nothing but their going is significant.

When people are, sore sick and at the point of death, sometimes their spirit is not able to depart when loved ones are around their bedside like the husband or the wife or even children nearer the bedside. They may ask the one to go and buy something for them or go to the next room and pick something for them. By the time they come back, the person is gone. At that point, what did the dying one experienced? Some will also die in presence of a bosom friend. When people are about to die, especially those who keep long in illness, what happens to them in their moments of departure? Are they in body or in spirit? Do they see some spiritual being ready for them, and do they converse as to send others away so that their spirit can leave the body, or the spirit of the sick is already gone? We may not know we cannot tell but we believe.

In many parts of the world people confessed the evils, they have committed before they die, especially those who went to church but committed evil. A minister was called to pray for a church member, who was dying. By the time, the minister got there, relatives were guarding the door. A relative refused the minister from going into the room. This minister out of curiosity forced his way through the door because he was a short person and his height helped him. To his amazement, the mouth of the dying man had been covered with a good piece of clothes so that he does not speak anymore. This was because, what the man was confessing was unbelievable and full of evil done against his own kinsmen. Medics might name the situation with medical terminologies, but to the traditional people, they are the real spiritual crimes committed because of visitations to various shrines or occults. Another elder of the church who was suddenly caught up with death out of fear of hell, started confessing his spiritual misdeeds. "God forgive me' he said, those I have killed when I was a driver, because they caused me trouble, those I have…." Then a relative shouted at him, "stop it" what is all this that you are talking about? The man kept quiet. We may not know we cannot tell, what record of criminal secrets people in many traditional areas hold within their brains, secret to them and their God, but we believe. This man died sometime later but if what he said was true, then what a burden church members who do no repent may carry to their graves.

Other families who are rich or have reputation in the community, sometimes seek assistance to sort out the sick person to die, than to allow the person to go on revealing evil secrets to disgrace the reputation of the family. In this way, "The evil that some people do secretly, chase after them publicly, before they die." Before they go to the grave, their deeds come to light before they die, and some spiritual evils others do, may not go to the grave without announcements of confessions of what they have done. A woman who was about to die, confessed her spiritual evil against a niece who stayed with her. The girl was very brilliant but was always very lean. She was in that condition throughout her education. Always seen as very lean. This auntie got ill and before she died, she confessed her spiritual deeds against her family. Among her victims was this young innocent girl who was staying with her. The auntie confessed she was the cause of the girls, leanness because she spiritually uses the girl's blood. That was why she was always very lean. After the death of the auntie, this lady became healthy with her natural body and there was no one in the community who had beautiful legs like hers, but because of her skinny situation the beauty of her legs was not seen. We may not know we cannot tell, whether some people can drain blood spiritually from their relatives, and for what? But we believe. It can happen that they use the blood spiritually for fuel or petrol for their spiritual travels but we may not know we cannot tell.

Another instance is that of stories about the death of witches. A man who was struggling in life was told by the mother not to sleep but to keep watch in the night. The mother told the son that he was going to see some three millipedes crawling into his room at night but forewarned the son not to kill the first millipede, but to kill the second and the third ones. The young man waited and true to his mother's word, he saw the three millipedes crawling towards his bed. Out of fear, he killed them all. He heard his mother shout, "Akwasi, you have killed me." The next morning he went to his mother and she was sick in bed and died later together with other two women in the village. What has the crawling millipedes had to do with the spirit of the women who died? We may not know we cannot tell, but we believe.

There was a Christian open-air revival in a town. The evangelist showed a film of cannibals or people who ate human flesh to show how witches eat human flesh spiritually. He then cursed all the witches and cautioned the queen of witches not to fly. After a week when the evangelist and his team were gone, an old woman in the town who was assumed to be the queen mother of the witches started bidding farewell to relatives and friends that she was going to travel. All those to whom she bid farewell thought she was traveling to visit her children who were in the city. On that fateful evening, she bid fare well to her nearest relative because the lorries left the town at dawn to the cities. In the morning, the old woman was dead. According to eyewitnesses, the old woman was dressed in bed as if she was travelling. She had apparently had her bath very late that night, put on her white neat cloth and slept peacefully to death. Medically it could be proved about the cause of her death to be a natural death, but then why did she bid farewell to people and why did she have her bath and dress and lie down and was gone, and in what way did she move out from her spirit and never return to her body? We may not know we cannot tell but we believe.

In the mid - nineties, One of the social paper's "People and Places" P&P, reported of a bird which had turned into a human form. A community of fishermen were sleeping outside their house near the beach because of the heat in their rooms at night. They suddenly heard a big splash of a bird which had collapsed on one of the children who were sleeping near the beach with the elderly. On hearing the noise and the child's cry they woke up only to see this large bird. The size of the bird amazed the fishermen and they tied the bird with a rope to drag it away when the bird suddenly turned into an old woman in her late seventies. Apparently this was an old ill person who was housebound because of her illness and weakness. This woman was then missing when she appeared by the seashore. We may not know we cannot tell, whether such stories are fabrications or real, but with this story, P&P came out with picture evidence for the public. Wonderfully created human beings, who can have power to be adverse spirituals in themselves. Wonderful creatures, wonderfully created as to create wonders. Aeroplanes in the skies have no ropes attached, yet wonderfully created humans make that happen. Ships in deep seas which do not sink. The great shark of submarines, which travels under water. No wonder, we may not know we cannot tell, but we believe, we have wonderfully, been created so as to fly away at death.

Chapter 5
AFTER DEATH

The spirit of the dead

Sympathisers who attended funerals in some traditional areas may have experienced the state whereby, the dead body, lying in state or about to be laid in the coffin, suddenly possessed someone, either a stranger, or a member of the family to communicate to relatives the reason of the death, or who killed him or her. Many are said to have revealed themselves to relatives to show them the place their dead bodies were, if they died and their bodies were missing. Some might accidentally have died in a bush or a thick forest, the spirit of the dead is able to locate people to the area through dreams or in a trance for relatives to find the body. We may not know, we cannot not tell, yet we believe they have happened and continue to happen.

The church to an extent, has achieved her goal in the Christian faith, over ghosts and their activities as the light of the gospel shone in places where darkness had reigned. In some communities, people stilled pay attention to ghosts and continue to attend church. There are those who leave food for ghosts or dead ancestors to eat. Some put water in jars on tables in their living room, in case a dead ancestors visited, they will have water to drink. The question of whether ghosts existed used to be a point of contention with the argument that when a person dies, that person is dead.

Psalm 146:4 "His breadth goes forth that very day" Many other Bible quotation confirm that the day a person dies, that one is dead. The traditional experience differ from the Bible. Referring to the witch at Endor to whom King Saul required of the ghost of Samuel, many traditional people are convinced, and confirms the traditional assumption that ghosts really exists.

The stories of ghosts as told in newspapers years back have gone down because of the teachings of the church and the strong belief of faith in God more than putting their trust in the things of the dead. The primary assertion of believers of God is that ghosts are activities of witches or unclean and familiar spirits, and that there are no real ghosts. Anything ones see about a dead person is of witches, or spirits because the dead are dead and gone.

Familiar spirits are those spirits within family linage to whom people have been born and died. These spirits are familiar with the life history of people. They know their voice. They have their picture. They can appear in their form like exactly the figure of the dead. How can one not believe? Why is it that for a long time people might not believe in such things, but on the day one voices out their unbelief or dare challenge the non- existence of such ghosts, the spirit of the dead will soon reveal themselves to such people to, but why at that time in particular? A young man whose father had been dead for more than twenty years never saw the ghost of his father. One day he spoke about it that there were no ghost and the he had never seen his father's ghost since he died. That very night, according to this young man, his legs seemed to be hanging in the skies when he was falling into deep sleep. He could not sleep well that night. Was it the ghost of his father or a witch or familiar spirit was at work, and why not previously but until that day. We may not know we cannot tell, but we believe.

This brings stories related to ghosts, which have also been diffused by certain events which have taken place in some places. There are beliefs of the spirit or the ghost of premature death people who becomes reckless or restless unless some rituals are performed for them to rest. This has been a long time belief whereby rituals are performed at places of accidents or where people had their untimely deaths to have drawn the soul or the spirit of the death away from where they are believed to have been stocked when they died, before they could move away. Rituals not performed could result in disturbances by the spirit of the dead person, to people in that area or the community or even strangers seeing the ghost of the person quite often. Some will board lorries, but at the time of destination, they are not found among the passengers and they do it so vividly that people witness their presence and absence.

Two instances of diffused ghost stories are the story of a pregnant woman who was knocked down by a vehicle and died on the spot. After few days later, people saw the ghost of this woman in the public toilet of the community at dawn. The ghost was seen either coming out from the male toilet or going into the female toilet in her shroud. This became a gossip in the community that the ghost of the death woman was disturbing people and causing fear among the people in the town. One day it happened that a young man was visiting the toilet at dawn just before daybreak and he saw the ghost in her shroud going into the male toilet or the gents. This young man was one who was known for his boozing with alcohol.

The young man shouted at the ghost and mentioned the name of the deceased woman and cautioned her to leave the community alone. Angry at the appearance of the ghost, the young man rushed to the toilet to tell the ghost that if she is dead, she stay calm in her grave and should stop disturbing the community, and more so why does she not attend the female toilets all the time but the male toilet. As soon as this young man got the boldness in himself against the ghost, the ghost turned from going to the male toilet and made for the female toilet. The young man at this time was angry with the ghost so he chased the ghost to the female toilet. It was then the ghost turned to the path leading to the town. The young man, still very courageous made his way after the ghost in her shrouded white robe. The young man overcame the ghost in a chase and gave her a slap. All of a sudden, the ghost turned to an old woman in the community who was known to the young alcoholic man. The woman asked him why he had slapped her and that she was going to report the young man to the chief at the palace. The young man said, "So it is you who have been doing this atrocity in the community. Go and report to the chief and I will come and answer" That was the end of the story and the end of the disturbances from the ghost to the toilet. The ghost was real a living human who used her unclean spirit to haunt the community in the form of a ghost. This will could be called a witchcraft acting with a familiar spirit.

In another incident, a man's wife died. After the burial, he was asked to observe the traditional rituals of widowhood rites because by the death of his wife he had become a widower. The man said there was no need of it and more so he was a Christian. People told him that if he did not observe the widowhood rite, the spirit of his wife might not leave him in peace and would disturb him. In most cases, the women will be persuading people into such things. The men mostly may not care about such things except they are prompted by the elders of the community to be breaching traditional rules.

Apart from that, the women will drag people into such things. Women believe in everything both in God and in other things including traditional rituals, which men may not care about. The widower did not observe the rites of widowhood for men.

One night as the widower lay sleeping, something made him woke up out from his sleep. There and then was standing before him his dead wife, dressed in the beautiful shroud she was laid in state with. The man out sorrow of the loss of his love one, his loneliness and the love to have his wife back, he boldly rose from the bed and embraced the ghost wife. To his amazement, the ghost immediately turned to the old woman who has been visiting the family after the death of the wife. The man became astounded. The woman begged him not to disgrace her. The man vowed never, ever to believe in ghost stories. They are real human beings with supernatural powers of familiar spirits who do such things. He saw them rather to be humans who have the craft of being witches. They have the potential to take up the portrait of the dead person to perform scenes to humanity. We may not know we cannot tell. We may agree to the assertion of some Christians that ghosts are not real but activities of evil people. Again this may further be argued by someone who has really seen a ghost, moved together, stayed together, ate and slept together. People's stories may be seen as real as they experienced and that makes it still difficult to convince others of the experience. We may not know we cannot tell, but we believe human beings are spirits as well.

Jesus's body after the resurrection.

From the Christian point of view, the difference of Jesus not being a ghost was that he appeared to people, he was seen by more than three hundred people which no ghosts have ever done and would not do. Earlier in his resurrection, he would not allow Mary to touch him because he had not been to his father. He later allowed himself to be touched by Thomas but his body did not vanish, until he had finished speaking to the disciples. This preceded having revealed himself to the disciples on the road to Emmaus. In John chapter 21, Jesus ate and questioned Peter whether Peter loved him. Finally he commanded his disciples to go and preach the gospel to all people and went up before their eyes. It would have been expected for real ghosts, to do one quarter of these to prove their existence.

> ***John 21: 1ff. "Afterwards, Jesus appeared again to his disciples, by the sea of Tiberius. It happened this way ... Early in the morning, Jesus stood on the shore, but the disciples did not realise, it was Jesus...."***
>
> ***Matthew 28: 19-21. Then Jesus came to them and said to them. All authority in heaven and on earth has been given to me. Therefore go and make disciples of all nations, baptizing them in the name of the Father and of the Son and of the Holy Spirit."***

Paul later received from Jesus what the apostles had witnessed concerning the Lord's Supper.

> ***I Corinthians 11:23-24. "For I received from the Lord what I also pass on to you", The Lord Jesus, on the night he was betrayed, took bread, and when he had given thanks, broke it, and said, "This is my body which is for you, do this in remembrance of me."***

There is no way one could argue that Jesus was a ghost after his resurrection. He was in a physical form more than a spirit ghost.

Traditions have stories of people who died and were met in other places residing and having children. Some lived and had a livelihood until a member of the family or someone who knew the person to be dead met him or her, or came to see the place of abode and then the living dead person disappears and is seen no more. The question we may not get an answer to is: where have the ghosts gone within our modern world of today? Or people no more have time for them or their activities and stories. Is it because of enlightenment and power of God is more than it was in times past. More Christians may be ready to confront with prayer and casting out or rebuking the spirit involved. If there they are humans working out from the powers they hold to, then they dare not expose themselves, for fear of being disgraced by the spirit of God, for which many have come under the anointing power of God to rebuke the devil and to cast out demons. More people have been educated than before .Though it is totally, not out of human settlement, people easily forget about these and move on with their lives after death.

Technology of our present world occupies people's minds more than thinking about ghosts. People are busier with life than before. Education and civilization has gone far with many developments in more places than before and moreover, many have turned to the Lord Jesus and are seriously seeking God in all things. This and many others have brought down some of these beliefs as they have been in days past. We may not know we cannot tell, but we believe ghosts still reveal themselves to areas where people are in the darkness of the gospel of Jesus Christ or still behind modern world.

Chapter 6

ENQUIRIES AFTER DEATH

Up to the modern day, ma ny traditions have not as yet fully accepted or refuse to understand death with scientific pathological explanations. The traditional beliefs of the spirit of the dead being able to reveal the reason of their death continue to be held by many people. Soothsayers have played the role of enquiring from the spirit of the dead from times of old. Some families continue to be enquiring about the death of their relatives especially when the death was so sudden. These range from accidents or long illness of painful diseases. We read from the Bible about King Saul and the witch at Endor in the first book of Samuel.

What the witch at Endor told King Saul came true.

Enquiries equally go with solutions and throwing back the evil to the sender or getting help in preventing such occurrence in the family. Just as families go for enquiries from soothsayers in the same way those who perpetuated the death also go to soothsayers for potent traditional medicines to ward off the spirit of the dead from disturbing them or retaliating for their death. Some go for traditional baths, or use of "talisman" to ward off the spirit of the dead victim. Some of these medicines would be planted on the graves of their dead victims secretly at night to lose the potency of the spirit of the dead from disturbing the culprits. The medicine in the power of plants is able to do in some way what these enquiries ask for.

At times the spirits who are bent to retaliate are able to deal with their culprits and cause their deaths as well. To such culprits, either they did not protect themselves from the power of the death spirit of their victim or the spirit of the dead victim became too powerful for them. Such spirits who are strong for their culprits are said to move away from their graves at night to elude planting on them such medicines on their graves to weaken them. In such case, the spirit of the dead becomes a disturbing spirit, who gives soothsayers the job of arresting such death spirits, with their spiritual powers and makes them 'rest in peace,' The belief and actions of such spirits of the death is that, they will not rest until they have spiritually avenged on their culprits and for the number of times they may be chasing their culprits out from their hide outs. The spirit of the said dead would cause havoc in the family until something is done before the dead spirit rests. We may not know we cannot tell whether it is the actual spirit of the dead or a human hand in them to work against the culprit.

The chief palace is where culprits can confess their evil, and rites done by slaughtering of sheep and pouring of libations to appease the death spirit and the case will have been dealt with.

The spirit of the dead after this has no right in the spirit of tradition to cause any more havoc after these rites have been performed. The spirit of the dead, then go to sleep and rest in an 'avenged' peace. At least the culprits who caused their deaths have then been exposed, and has become a shame on them or a disgrace to the family. This have been happening in many traditional areas. We may not know we cannot tell but we believe.

The truth and the fallacy of soothsayers

Soothsayers sometimes have conflicting reports of the cause of the death of one particular person. At times, families may go to consult soothsayers for the cause of the death if the families are not on good terms. When this happens both families may go to different soothsayers and might be bringing different and sometimes conflicting reports. If the partner of the deceased is a very rich person, the first soothsayer might say the deceased has been used for ritual purposes for more money. At the same time the other party would be told by another soothsayer that the dead woman had gone against a taboo and she has died as a result. The interesting thing is that none of the party is able to officially confront the one whom the soothsayer accused of crime, but it will be rumoured as an open secret. It is only in special cases in which such inquires result in the chief palace for one to swear an oath of innocence in the death of the relative. If the one who is alleged to have spiritually caused the death hears of the rumours, the only thing he or she can do is to go to the chief's palace and deny the rumours. This would be proofed by the elders giving a plant concoction prepared by a fetish priest which has the potential of proofing people true of accusations or not. We may not know we cannot tell. This medicinal concoction is a mixture of some black substances with eggs by the fetish priest, and the concoction is given to the one to drink as a proof. The drinking is accompanied by curses pronounced by the one drinking the stuff. If nothing happens to the person after that, at least a week or two, it becomes a traditional divine proof that the one is innocent.

Some also become ill as to confess what they had done. We may not know, we cannot tell, the potency of the fetish medicine on the health of the one drinking it at that time, and if the one became sick whether the medicine might have trickled a hidden disease in the person or not, the belief is that as far as the person was the culprit, the one became sick and died or something else happened to that person.

We can medically agree with the Bible prohibitions of such things for the Christians. If the potency of such fetish medicine causes medical problem to the person who is made to drink the concoction, how can they medically convince the people that the culprit in the eyes of the people is now a victim of drinking something to which the body has an allergy to, or has reacted to the medicine? This person might psychologically die of disgrace. For being given a name that does not belong to him or her but for the person to clear his or her name with rumours, he has bought his own death medically. We may not know we cannot tell, but we believe.

The separate dwelling on the soothsayers or fetish priests, and the different versions from the different places at times, makes it difficult for some people to believe all that they hear. In the olden days, some relatives of the dead were given cutlass or sharp knives to kill their culprits if they were the cause of their deaths. These spirits go and perform the work; others also go to rest from "this war" with their culprits. At times there may be someone in the family who has been consulting fetish priests and other spiritualists to cause the death of other family members. These same spiritualists become the killer of lives in the community and turn run to tell their consultants who killed their relatives, thus diverting the real case elsewhere.

Chapter 7

STORIES ABOUT THE DEATH

Many traditions have stories to tell about the dead. They may be unbelievable, yet they do happen. There was the story of a promising lady who died prematurely. The death was initially associated with a man she was going out with; another version of the cause of the death was associated with a woman she quarrelled with. All these were believed by people as the cause of her death. Another man died in the same town. His death was attributed to a friend who killed him through a curse. People believed the cause of the death from the rumours they heard. Other deaths followed and the deaths were equally attributed to people to have caused the death. Long after these deaths, a dying man who was well known in the town confessed the evils he had committed against the people in that area, through the occult. Out of his confessions he mentioned the name one of his victims to be the lady who died and her death was attributed to someone else. The man again mentioned other people he had equally killed by sending them to fetish priests and spirits to kill them through the occult. Meanwhile these deaths had already been hanged on other people's necks to have caused the deaths. Another woman also confessed whilst she was dying about people she has killed through the same way by travelling to places to cause the deaths of those people who had caused her anger either through struggling for property or stealing her properties. This brings the mystery of death and the reason given and sources of the seer who predicts the culprit whom people think might have caused the death until a later confession. Notwithstanding people really die of curses inflicted on them by their causers who do these through the fetish occults. Some are also known to have really caused the death after they are seen going for traditional medicines to bathe to ward off the spirit of the dead after the burial takes place.

Satan is a deceiver. If the Bible says we should not put our trust in such things, it is true. Again in many traditions, no one dies without attributing the death to somebody or something that might have gone bad with the person. Wives of late, have traditionally been exonerated by bereaved relatives of the deceased, for being the cause of their husband's deaths when laws on inter-estate succession were implemented. If children now inherit their fathers, then the wife is traditionally cleared not to have killed the husband. If not, then what was the traditional reason for the distress which many widows went through by the dead man's relatives whilst the property was to be inherited by relatives of the husband? This goes on to show the deceits of evil and the lack of the rule of proper laws which defended such vulnerable widows in many areas of our world. People who through the occult kill and do many spiritual atrocities will turn round and put the blame on those who have no one to stand up for them. Again using the same women as tools, these same women in the name of sisters of the dead man will hail insults on their fellow woman who has lost her husband. As they hail the insults, they turn to be taking things out of the house of their deceased brother or relative. Now that the relative is dead, they have a say in the affairs of the marriage. The blindness of traditions for time past has been a woe and short sightedness to most communities. The greediness of people coupled with envy and jealousy have made many children of the deceased to be cut off from their future aspirations and careers. Many children never rose to their places in society when their fathers were taken away from them. Upon all the insults and the hard treatments their mothers went through with them, not many family relatives did care for them in the name of their late brother or the property they inherited. As to the envies and greediness of family relatives of old, we may not know we cannot tell, how families have been destroyed and the bright future of many people in various communities. How many people may have been affected, not counting on their progress in life alone, but with their brilliant contribution and promising years which never materialised because of the death of their parents, but we believe.

Chapter 8
THE GHOST OF THE PROPHET SAMUEL

1st Samuel 28: 1ff.

When Samuel the prophet died, King Saul was very upset when he did not receive any message from the Lord. He inquired from a witch or a medium in a town by name Endor. King Saul asked the witch to call the spirit of the late prophet Samuel for enquiry about his situation. This was because King Saul the King wanted to know the outcome a war ahead and whether he was going to win the war or not. Whether the King was going to come out safely from the war or die. When the witch saw (the ghost of) Samuel, she shouted at King Saul who had then disguised himself. This was because the king had previously commanded all the witches to be killed and that particular witch had escaped. The prophet Samuel used to give the King messages from God whilst he was alive. King Saul asked the medium, "what do you see? The woman said, **"I see a spirit coming out from the ground..., an old man wearing a robe is coming up." verse 13.** King Saul knew it was the ghost of the prophet Samuel.

Samuel asked Saul, **"Why have you disturbed me by bringing me up; why do you consult me, now that the Lord has turned away from you and become your enemy."** Then the ghost of Samuel went on to tell the king what was going to happen to him with the pending war the next day.

> ***Verse 17. "The Lord has done what he predicted through me, The Lord has torn the kingdom out of your hands and given it to one of your neighbours- To David.- Because you did not obey the Lord. The Lord will hand over both Israel and you to the hands of the Philistines, and tomorrow you and your sons will be with me."***

This meant that, King was going to die the following day likewise all his sons with him. It happened exactly as the spirit or the ghost of Samuel told King Saul. The king died in war with his sons the following day and Israel was defeated by the Philistines.

Now, what was the meaning of the spirit of the late Samuel which came out from the ground? Did it mean that God had not taken Samuel away?

This is what the apostle John saw on the island of Patmos.

> ***Revelation 6:9-11 "When he opened the fifth seal, I saw under the altar the souls of those who had been slain for the word of God and for the witness they had borne. They cried out with a loud voice, 'O Sovereign Lord, holy and true, how long before you will judge and avenge our blood on those who dwell on the earth? And they were each given a white robe, and told to rest a little longer, until the number of their fellow saints and their brothers should be complete, who were to be killed as they themselves had been."***

Should some Godly saints be kept by God and others allowed to be disturbed?

Again all that the spirit told the king through the medium happened the following day. Are there spirits in the realm of death who equally know what is going to happen to the realms of the living as to reveal secrets when invoked? Was that ghost the real spirit of the dead prophet Samuel or another familiar spirit taking the form of Samuel to reveal the future of the King and the outcome of the war? In this case those who consult the spirit of dead relatives and get convinced with what they are told, could be right with their conviction, but from which spiritual source? God or satanic?

Jude. Verse 9 "But when the archangel Michael, contending with the devil, was disputing about the body of Moses, he did not presume to pronounce a blasphemous judgement, but said, 'the Lord rebuke you."

If Satan had an access to the dead body of Moses, what would Satan had done with the spirit of Moses amongst the Israelites? Nowhere in the Bible was the ghost of Moses seen or consulted by the people of Israel. God would equally not have given the body of the prophet Samuel to be used in this way. Familiar spirits were at work. They equally know future events the history of people.

> ***Deuteronomy 18:10, "When you reach the land of Lord your God is giving you, do not learn to imitate, the detestable ways of the nation's there. Let no one be found among you who sacrifices his son or daughter in the fire, who practices divination, or sorcery, interprets omens, engages in witchcraft or casts spells, or is a medium or spiritualist."***

> ***Verse 12 "Anyone who does these things is detestable to the Lord. And because of these detestable practises, the Lord your God will drive out those nations before you."***

> ***Verse. 14 "The nations you will dispossess listen to those who practice sorcery or divination."***

Traditional beliefs have a cause for what they believe. They know what they talk about when they say there are ghosts of dead ancestors. Unlike the Bible, the traditional belief, **"seeing is believing"** is just opposite of what the Bible say about belief. In the secular world many mysteries happen for people to fully believe in what they say. For example, for Okomfo Anokye in Ghana to have invoked a golden stool to have descended from the skies is a positive belief. This golden stool has been kept up to this day by the Ashantis of Ghana and is a vivid evidence. In the same way ghosts are real to the traditionalist. Sometimes when people die, relatives see them in dreams and communication takes place either about their condition in the land of the dead. Sometimes they are seen to be still ill especially during the early weeks of their death. Later they appear beautiful and full of life in them though they may be dead. In all these, are they true spirits in the sight of God to be doing such revelations, and if so why did God restrict the people of Israel not to be involved with such practices? We may not know we cannot tell, but we believe angels have not been given such assignments by God. The rebellion of Satan continues against God, using spirit beings as the army of rebels.

Between the dead and their activities, there are instances where people who were bold to confront ghosts also saw living humans who had taken the form of the dead person to parade in the name of the death person. As narrated above, the man who boldly embraced the ghost of his deceased wife only saw a human being. Again, in the case of the ghost, who was hunting people at a public toilet, it turned out to be another human being. We may not know we cannot tell, whether those who have evidence like king Saul and Samuel's ghost, would believe in ghosts, but we believe the Bible does not adhere to such, since demons can easily take human forms and parade like ghosts. There was a struggle between Satan and the angel Michael over Moses dead body. We may not know we cannot tell, what Satan might have done with Moses spirit if he had had an access to it, and nowhere in the Bible did we hear of the ghost of Moses parading amongst the Israelites even though they continued in the wilderness with the pillar of fire and cloud before and after them. Moses ghost never appeared in the congregation of Israel for the people to believe in Moses' ghost. Jesus revealing himself to his disciples challenged them that he was not a ghost because a ghost does not eat fish or bread or breakfast, except traditional belief in ghosts, and they are placed with food and jugs for them to eat and drink when they visit their families in ghost form.

The dead can appear in the dreams of a loved one. We may not know we cannot tell, but some appearance of the spirit of some dead person to their relatives to give directions or gave them something resulted in the good for such relative to have named their children after the dead spirit or ghost as 'good ghost' or 'Samanpa' for the Akan's in Ghana. The church is silent on such as to not allow people to put their faith or trust in such things, but spirits of dead which sometimes appear in dreams try to show to humanity that the dead are in a different state of the realm of spirits.

Arguments for and against the appearance of ghosts stem from many things Satan can do to deceive people. In God we trust.

Chapter 9

FUNERALS

Rest in Peace

"Rest in peace", the dead are bid a farewell. Burial graves are engraved with the initials. 'RIP' for most of the dead who are buried in cemeteries. Both rich and poor, famous and unknown, young and old, wicked and the good are bid to rest in peace by loved ones. We may not know we cannot tell whether some rest at all, and let alone ' in peace' , or those who actually rest in peace and those who do not. Rest is rest and peace is peace, yet sometimes resting with peace can be disturbed with inconveniences or intruders. One's rest or sleep can be disrupted when the mind is wondering or worrying about other things. One's peace can be disturbed when others make him or her uncomfortable with noise whilst sleeping. The dead can rest, but as to be resting in peace is another question. People rest, yet they cannot sleep. People die but the atrocities they caused humanity when they were alive, can deprive their peace to rest.

Traditions have many stories of people who went down to the land of the dead, and they had no place amongst their own dead ancestors or dead people in the land of the dead, because of their evil deeds whilst they lived. Some were forced to confess their evil deeds before they died. For others, death would not take them away and for some, the dead refused them place of abode even to take them away. We may not know we cannot tell, what happens when wicked people die. Do they rest in peace? Can a person who has killed many people rest in peace when he goes to meet all whom he had killed whilst on earth, if there really exists the land of the dead where the dead reside? What about corpses who are given knives to pay back those who caused their death before they sleep or rest. What about if they do not get their victims. Would they rest in peace when the living culprits also fortify themselves with super ghost powers against the spirit of the dead? Would the dead continue to hunt until their culprits die, and would they fight them, or are the dead not allowed to do such things in order to rest? People who believe in the activities of the dead do consult the dead for many things. Others go to the cemetery to call the spirits of the dead. If all these work then can the dead rest in peace? There is a mysterious story of someone who died and something made the family exhume the body after two days only to see the dead body turned upside down, stripped off his clothes and lashed till the back skin was full of the marks of the whip. We may not know we cannot tell, whether people exhumed the body and lashed him or the dead was lashed in the land of the dead but we believe some dead people do rest in peace and others may not rest at all if they really do meet those they offended.

The story of Lazarus and the rich man in Luke 19, depicts a scene. A poor man dies. A poor man is buried with a poor burial. Some poor people could have been refused burial because they had no money for a nice burial or their relatives were also poor, but for the reason that the poor dead body should be buried, they will by all means go to the grave because they no more fit in the land of the living. This poor man is buried without popularity. On the other hand, a rich man dies. The entire town is moved with friends and relatives going up and down to present a "one in town burial" which may be next to a state burial. A church service with a difference, drawing crowds on one side and few at the other side, which was not popular as to deserve a rich burial. Biography and tribute of a great difference. The rich man has a nice brochure of beautiful print with portraits all over the place. The poor man has not many friends. As the saying goes "poor no friend." Friends of the rich man write tributes upon tributes, pictures of the dead man on the streets. A mass of people may follow up to the cemetery, cars upon cars, which follow the hearse, family members and many friends. "Oh the funeral was big," they will say. Rest in perfect peace said more than a hundred times, whilst the poor man had only one. Very rich grave laid with ceramic tiles. The poor man is buried in the ordinary mud grave. The funeral continues. Who would ever think of such a rich person, like Dave in the New Testament, to have opened his eyes and being tormented in the flame despite the rich popular funeral? Where is Rest, Peace, and Perfect peace? We may not know we cannot tell, but death and the aftermath will continue to be a mystery for all people on the earth. It will therefore be good for people to choose the real life before they died. This real life is accepting Jesus Christ as one's Lord and Saviour and living a life which is pleasing in his sight.

In hell, the rich man wanted Abraham to send someone to his five brothers and warn them of the truth of the matter after death. What Abraham told the dead rich man continues with humanity, ***"we have many Moses or leaders of various churches and the prophets. If they will not obey them, they will equally not obey anyone who goes out from here."***

The Bible says, ***"Blessed are those who die in the Lord, for they rest from their labours"***

This may be one of the causes we give rest to the dead for their toils and labours on earth. What is it to rest from one's labour after one dies in the Lord? What is the labour, worldly labour, or godly labour, and in what way? What about others who did not die in the lord? What about Christians who did not finish their labour on earth? Are such Christians going to continue their work after death? Would there be rest for them then? We may not know we cannot tell, but we believe. Paul prayed for Timothy" that he may fulfil his ministry.

Chapter 10

THOSE WHO RESTED AFTER DEATH

Samuel the prophet died and rested. David died and rested. All the apostles finished their work and rested. Is there rest for the ungodly after death? we may not know we cannot tell, but we believe. Christians should finish their work and rest in death, than to rest supplementary rest, where one would have to continue working in the land of the death if that is true at all. According to the bible, Jesus went and preached to the dead in the land of the dead. 1 Peter 3:18-19

1 Peter 4:6 "He finally sits at the hand of God till all are subdued under his feet" If that was so, then it may mean some will rest from their labours whilst others will continue working if they did not finish their work? Again if this is so, then Christians should strive to finish their work or fulfil their ministry. We may not know we cannot tell but we believe.

At funeral services, burial sentences may be said, ***"The Lord giveth, the Lord has taken away; Blessed be the name of the Lord"***

Which of the deaths does the Lord take away and which of them do people take away? Death by illness, curses perpetuated by evil spirits, wars or crimes against humanity, or by negligence? We may not know we cannot tell, but we believe the dead will be divided between God and Satan. Those who die in the Lord will be taken by God, and Satan will take the rest who did not die in the Lord and did not know God.

Chapter 11
BIOGRAPHY AND TRIBUTES

Saint Paul says "our lives are like a letter being written." At the end of the day, the envelope is removed and the letter sent to the owner of the body. Reading of biographies at death shows a picture of the dead person. The day born and life led. We may not know we cannot tell why all the dead biographies depicts good and lovely people whilst we live amongst greed and social vices all the time. No family have ever said wrong about their dead relative. Where are the negatives written and where are they to be read? At the family house, at the graveside, or by the dead themselves, we may not know we cannot tell, but we believe bad things are not to be said about the dead. Yet people have committed serious offences and were praised after death. We do so to the dead, because death is painful to every family and saying bad things about their dead will be like casting their love one to hell. That is not our duty. We may not know we cannot tell, but we believe, we will say the good they did and God will unveil the rest at the judgement day.

There is a church who has cancelled reading of tributes of their dead members. This may come as news to many but they do not read tributes of the deceased. The truths of tributes people give about their dead may be questionable. Many dead, if they were given the chance to speak would tell the gathering of mourners whether what is being said of them is true or false. The reason people say only good things about their dead may be a fear that the spirit of the dead will do something against them. Why we cannot say bad things about people in death, we may not know we cannot tell, but we believe it is a disgrace and moreover every family wants good for their loved ones especially for them to go to heaven. Why then tell of their wrong doings? The judge is God. Yet, there are many dead people who have really troubled others whilst they lived yet they all had good tributes. Mark them correct.

A young girl died. People in the neighbourhood knew that she was insolent and disrespectful. Tributes given to her were that she was a good girl. After the burial, some people in the neighbourhood quietly gossiped that the tributes were not said as to the real person the dead young girl was. Most people do receive good and nice tributes though people know them to be otherwise. What makes people give good tributes to dead relatives though they might not be all that? We believe during their life time they had their good side and their bad side so the bad side is hidden at death and the good side revealed to transport to God. God himself is given the responsibility to fish the bad side from his books and not man. We may not know we cannot tell. But we believe.

DEATH AND INTELLECTS

We may not know we cannot tell, the value of brains which go into the grave at death. Counting on the death of intellectuals, wise people, politicians, clergy and many more. We may not know we cannot tell, but we believe. Intellectual brains of wisdom have gone down into the grave. Such brains could be have been collected at death and kept for those who are not wise. We may not know we cannot tell, but we believe, books have been written to keep some brains, and those who do not have can look for them in the books.

Chapter 12
THE MYSTERY OF SAINTS

Church saints

The word "saint" has religiously been used for a long time for spirituality and the dead. Saint Augustine, Saint Anthony etc. The other use of the word saints has been wrongly used for the calling of spirits which are really not saints before God but demons or familiar spirits who come to work for people and possess them at the same time to destroy them. Many African students have been victims of calling on such saints for passing of examinations or learning to be 'break.' Books written for the calling of saints which should have otherwise been renamed, have deceptively been portrayed as books of light where people can follow instructions to receive power for help. We may not know we cannot tell, how saints in these ways have deceptively destroyed the human spirit of many people.

In the Bible, Paul easily called the members of the church 'Saints' in his opening letters, Paul addresses the Ephesian Christian's as saints.

"To the saints who are in Ephesus, and are faithful in Christ Jesus: Grace to you and peace from God our Father and the Lord Jesus Christ."

If Paul calls Christians saints, then the word 'saints' should still continue for the latter Christian churches so that members would live like saints or be saintly.

Chapter 13

CEMETERY SAINTS

We may not know we cannot tell what the saints are doing at the cemetery. *"And I heard a voice from heaven saying, 'Blessed are the dead who die in the Lord, for they rest from their labour'." Revelation.14:13*

In the event of the dead Prophet, Samuel being awoken from his grave by a witch or a diviner at the request of King Saul. What the spirit of the prophet Samuel told the king, happened to him, it did happen. If such was from God, then why did God initially command the elimination of the witches or diviners from the land? This particular witch had escaped and was still working as a diviner consultant. Samuel had lived on earth for just few years as compared to the ages of spirits who know history and past lives of people and future events.

Satan had wanted to gain hold of the body of Moses and an angel struggled with him until the angel rebuked Satan to let go.

> *Jude verse 9 "But even the archangel Michael, when he was disputing with the devil about the body of Moses, did not dare to bring a slanderous accusation against him, but he said, 'the Lord rebuke you'!"*

Whatever be the case, saints have nothing doing at the cemetery except that the dead are resting from their labour. The dead have no extra work to do for humankind as to receive consultations or surgery from the cemetery. This has for a long time been a spiritual demonic propaganda. They have lured innocent souls of the church into believing in demonic, and unholy saints. As a result such callers of saints have been possessed by various demons. These demons continue to be a threat in the lives of such callers unknowingly to them. They have become victims of demons as a result of calling saints at the cemetery or elsewhere. Some may not know, some cannot tell, but we, believe.

Chapter 14

GODLY DEAD SAINTS

These are the dead in the Lord. By calling them saints, does not mean they have become spirits to be consulted. They are only faithful church members or Christians who have died in the Lord Jesus Christ. These are who we call the church triumphant. Christians who are alive are the church militant as we continue to war with sin, the flesh and Satan. In death, they are the saints of God who have triumphed.

> *Rev. 14 "Blessed are those who are the dead in the Lord from now on," Says the spirit "that they may rest from their labours, for their deeds follow them."*
>
> *Hebrews 12:1-2a "Therefore since we are surrounded by so great a cloud of witnesses, let us also lay aside every weight, and sin which clings so closing, and let us run with endurance the race that is set before us, looking to Jesus, the founder and perfector of our faith."*

This cloud of witnesses are the saved ones who have died. They lived as saints and died as saints. There is no way the dead in Christ can rise up to help people or bring answers to their prayers. These are the works of the Holy Spirit. We remember them and gives thanks to God for their lives and what they achieved in their Christian journey. Remembering them does not allow for the calling of their spirits, if they can be found at all. Calling of dead as saints are demonic and the working of unclean spirits. Humans give demons more work to do for them in the name of saints of light but they are of darkness, whose dwellings are the pit of hell. Calling on such saints makes callers sign a bond of hell as their dwelling place with the spirits when they also die too become saints. This, we believe. Jesus promised the disciple who was going to help them. (The Holy Spirit)

John 14:16, "And I will ask the Father and he will give you another helper, to be with you forever."

In the Bible angels are named as angels or messengers of God and not saints.

Luke 1:26 "In the sixth month the angel Gabriel was sent from God to a city of Galilee Nazareth to a virgin betrothed to a man whose name was Joseph, of the house of David and the virgin's name was Mary."

We do not have Saint Gabriel or Saint Michael but rather Angel Gabriel and Angel Michael.

Daniel 8:16 "And I heard a man's voice between the banks of the Ulai, and it called, Gabriel, make this man understand the vision."

Verse 21 "While I was speaking in prayer, the man Gabriel, whom I had seen in the vision at the vision at the first, came to me in swift flight at the time of the evening sacrifice."

These angels are ministering angels and were sent by God to perform deeds for the people of God or to reveal his purpose. God sent angel Gabriel to Mary that she was going to conceive and bear a son.

In the calling of saints, some people call on names which may include the names of dead people or angels as well. Names mentioned as saints are names which does not exist in the Bible and if anything at all, Christians are not supposed to be calling on the names of dead people who have been named saints by humans. All believers must pray to the Lord for their need.

"Do not be anxious about anything, but in everything, by prayer and petition, with thanksgiving, present your requests to God." Philippians 4:6

Calling on names of the dead leads to necromancy Deuteronomy 18; 10

Calling on saints or spirits which one does not know may bring these things.

You do not know which spirit you are calling or the nature of that being, except by the name given. Saint Michael, Saint Anthony, Saint Martha.

Acts 3:16 "There is no name given under heaven by which we can be saved."

Matthew 1:21 "She will give birth to a son, and you are to give the name Jesus, because he will save his people from their sins."

"Luke 1:31 "You will be with child and give birth to a son, and you are to give him the name Jesus."

Chapter 15

UNCLEAN SAINTS

The calling of the spirit of Samuel by the witch of Endor is clear. A person with an unclean spirit cannot call on a clean spirit. An unclean spirit will respond to their agents who are working with the same unclean spirits. True Christian believers call on the Holy Spirit and the Holy Spirit responds to them. Unbelievers call on unclean spirits and the unclean spirits respond to them. A spirit which worked with the witch of Endor, came to replace the dead Samuel. Many who consult the spirit of the dead experience the same thing king Saul experienced and that does not make it godly spiritual. Calling of saints by church people is therefore questionable for any Christian believer. It is more the calling on unclean spirits or demons than God's Holy Spirit, and God does not like it.

We may not know we cannot tell, but we believe the use of the word 'saint' in the religious sense of the word, has gone a long way to deceive people and has contributed to spirits possession in many people who have called on saints, Spirit beings whose nature they did not know.

There is nowhere in the Bible the word of God allows Christians to invoke on the spirit of the dead as saints, or to invoke them in prayers or to seek saints from cemeteries or where the dead may be.

Demons come to work to deceive the callers as if a saint responded to their request. Satan has power to do that. Calling of saints is not biblical and we believe. People entangle themselves unconsciously with unclean spirits they do not know. These spirits come to possess their callers as well. Thus invokers of saints have within their spirits, evil saints.

Spiritual beings are still spirit beings. They equally know what is going to happen in the realm of the physical. They are not from God yet they feign to work on behalf of God. They are spiritual deceivers.

Deuteronomy 18; 9-13

"When you enter the land the Lord your God is giving you, do not learn to imitate the detestable ways of the nation's there. Let no one be found among you who sacrifices his son or daughter in the fire, who practices divination or sorcery, interprets omens, engages in witchcraft, or cast spells, or who is a medium or spiritist or who consults the dead. Anyone who does this is detestable to the Lord, and because of this detestable practice, your God will drive out those nations before you. You must be blameless before the Lord your God."

God does not want any of his people to be involved in such practices.

Many youths have been led into these spiritual practices whereby they call on spirits they do not know, in the name of saints to perform their wills for them. Most students are led into these practices to call upon saints to help them in their studies or for power to allow girls into their lives or for other things. Some adults do the same. Those who have indulged themselves in such practices have had problems within their spirits. This is because the saints they called upon when they were young are still with them unless they have given their lives to Christ and allowed themselves to be delivered out from the hands of these saints. The sad story is that most of such people might have now grown up and been in positions in society and therefore would not succumb to deliverance. Some will take it as they are already Christians with church positions, but the saints are still battling with them in their lives.

Many spiritual marriages of men whereby their marriages cannot stand may be their calling of saints if they ever had contacts with such spirits. Many people's Christianity has become a constant failure because the saints are still with them and because they are not from God, which makes it difficult for such people to lead the good Christian lives.

The names of saints are not as their consultants think. There are spirits, other than the spirit of God which appears to work for them. We may not know we cannot tell but we believe some people have achieved their purpose with such saint calling, but were they the saints from God or from the devil? If people do call saints and are friends of saints, then their lives would be saintly, and not destructive or against their fellow humans.

Chapter 16

THE MYSTERY OF THE AFTERLIFE

Heaven and hell

Where is heaven and where is hell? Where is purgatory? Where is the land of the dead ancestors? What if those who do not believe in God died and got to know in death that there was heaven and those who believed in God are taken there? Would they return to earth to believe and die again? ***"It is appointed unto man once to die and after that judgement"*** Why then, can they not see God if God existed before they died. If there was heaven where would they be and if there was hell where would they be, if they did not believe in Jesus to register their names in the heavenly salvation book of life whilst they lived? Could there be a later registration of names after death for their salvation? For this we know that people have their own self will to choose whom they would like serve. The mystery is within the afterlife. This is no gambling. It is a fearful thing to fall into the hands of the living God when one dies and there is actual heaven and actual hell. We may not know we cannot tell, but we believe some will weep and gnash their teeth, whilst others receive reward for their faith and works for God whilst on earth.

Chapter 17

The psalm '50' fool

Psalm 50:1, "A fool says in his heart there is no God"

Is this fool a fool whilst he or she is alive, or when he or she dies? We may not know we cannot tell but we believe. Will people weigh the gravity of their foolishness with a capital or small letter when they spend all their lives and die without God? We may not know we cannot tell. How true this scripture will be for some unbelievers.

> *Revelation 20:12-15 "Then I saw the dead, great and small, standing before the throne, and books were opened. Then another book was opened, which is the book of life. And the dead were judged by what was written in the books, according to what they had done. And the sea gave up the dead who were in it. Death and Hades gave up the deaths who were in them, and they were judged each one of them, according to what they had done. And Death and Hades were thrown into the lake of fire, And if any one name was not found written in the book of life, he was thrown into the lake of fire. Revelation 20:12-14*
>
> *This is the second death.*

What about those who know God, yet do not like walking in his ways? Those who follow teachings which might not necessary help them to obey God.

Matthew 7:21. "Not everyone who says to me, "Lord, Lord", will enter the kingdom of heaven."

In the parable of rich people, one rich man concentrated on his riches and failed to be kind to the poor.

The rich fool only concentrated on his business of getting more, saving more, and resting his soul at pension, but what would these things do to him at his death, apart from leaving inheritance for relatives who did not toil to inherit? What awaits the ungodly even though they know the light of the gospel, yet refuse to attend to it?

Romans 1:18-22 "For the wrath of God is revealed from heaven against all ungodliness and unrighteousness of men, who by their unrighteousness, supress the truth. For what can be known about God is plain to them, because God has shown it to them. For his invisible attributes, namely, his eternal power and divine nature, has been clearly perceived ever since the creation of the world, in the things that has been made. So they are without excuse, For although they knew God, they did not honour him as God or give thanks to him, but they became futile in their thinking, and their foolish hearts were darkened. Claiming to be wise, they became fools."

Does this fool equally affect the church member who does not do the will of God?

Matthew 7:7 "Truly, truly I say unto you, not all who call me Lord, Lord will enter into the kingdom of

heaven, but those who do the will of my Father who is in heaven. On that day, many will say to me, 'Lord, did we not prophesy in your name ,and cast out demons in your name, and od many mighty works in your name, And then I will declare to them,' I never knew you; depart from me, you workers of lawlessness."

The unbelievers may not bother about this. "Let us eat and drink", they may say; "for tomorrow we die." To the believers there is a caution of the way we may live, because of judgement in whatever we do, whether good or evil. To the ordinary church goer, it is a mystery. When they are asked about their salvation in Jesus Christ, many will say only "God knows." but 'Faith' is things unseen which we believe and hope for.

Hebrews 11:1 "Now faith is assurance of things hoped for, the conviction of things not seen."

Romans 1:17 "The just shall live by faith."

Hebrews 10:38 "But my righteous one shall live by faith, and if he shrinks back, my soul has no pleasure in him."

Chapter 18

THE MYSTERY OF THE 'BEINGS' CALLED HUMAN BEINGS

Human beings are mysterious in themselves. No coroner has seen the organ of speech when someone died. There is no organ which contains words we think or speak. The brain does not show thinking, except with some aspect of damage and speech becomes a problem. Human beings are mysterious when they die and refuse to open their eyes or respond to situations around them. Human beings are mysterious when they consciously move about in their spirit states to cause harm or consciously contain adverse spirits in their soul state. We were wonderfully created.

> *Genesis 1:26 "And God said, let us make man in our own image, after our likeness. And let them have dominion over the fish of the sea and over the birds of the heavens and over the livestock and over all the earth and over every creeping thing that creeps on the earth."*
>
> *Genesis 2:7. "And the Lord God formed man out from the dust of the ground, and breathed into his nostrils the breath of live, and man became a living being."*

Thus a new being was created with a body which was to live on the earth in the form of human beings with personalities. They are composed of body, soul and spirit. Unlike robots, they can speak, think and act. They moved about uncontrolled by any machine other than that of the breath of God which is the active force which makes them move and live and have their beings. This being who is human, is physical. This being can speak and relate.

Unlike animals these beings are different. They are creative. They can consciously harm and do good. They can produce materials which they use to harm and kill themselves in their bodily forms. They fight and war. They sing are become merry. They trade and make wealth.

Genesis 4: 20-22 "Adah bore Jabal; he was the father of those who dwell in tents and have livestock. His brother's name was Jubal; he was the father of all those who play the lyre and pipe. Zillah also bore Tubal-Cain. He was the forger of all instruments of bronze and iron."

This passages shows the first pioneers of trade or business and pioneers of inventions of instruments of war and music."

These beings, called human beings, are the stewards of the earth to keep and till the soil. In this way, these beings build houses for their earthly accommodation. Like ants, they plan their lifestyle with leadership. They are grouped across the earth with beauty and diversity of skin colour. Though there are over billions in number on the face of the earth, they are of different faces and they are identified by different names. They communicate their own languages and live in groups with dialects in areas where they are gathered, even though others learn such languages in order to move in same language groups. Since they were created a history of their creation has been kept for their remembrance as they are reproduced. This is to keep them on track with their creator God. Yet they try to know more about themselves, they enquire through research about their physical estate and try to find solutions to keep them alive and existing in their bodily form. Despite all their success with curing their bodies for good health, they grow old and become weak and die.

These beings are subject to their creator, yet they choose to serve their creator or not. Though they are supposed to be in relationship to their creator, some refuse to be in relationship with their creator God. Their creator always call on them through their counterparts who are in relationship with God, yet some still refuse. These beings called humans beings, know what is good and bad. Some choose the good, others become bad. Some kill, others hate whiles many choose to love. In a large world given to them by their creator, they have moral code of law and lifestyle which they should live as beings who are human because other creatures share nature as well. Some of the human beings do follow the moral code and others do not. Some go to the extent of destroying nature. Nature at times gets angry with them and attack them. The sea does carry many of them away with a fierce anger. The earth does opens her mouth and swallows some of them. The wind blows them off and sometimes nature sparks fire and burns their crops and places of abode. Nature does this because the wrongs human beings do causes nature to groan and also to vomit them out. Nature is older in creation than these 'beings' and stronger than human beings. These 'beings' called human beings, have limited time to live. They die and their bodies decay but their spirits live on.

Human beings are mysterious in creation. They can consciously be in relation with other spirit beings like their creator, for good and love or consciously merge with other bad spirit beings, to harm their fellow human beings. In the company of other beings who are not human, they do many things against the beings to cause harm and death. How these 'beings' in their bodily form, are able to relate with other non-personal 'beings' is sometimes mysterious to the 'beings' in their human form. Those who relate to the creator God in their human form, are able to relate to the Holy Spirit of God who is in harmony with the creator God. Through the Holy Spirit these receive help against the other 'beings' who cause them trouble in the body form.

Again these beings are created as human spirit beings who dwell in the tabernacle of the physical body.

> ***2 Corinthians 5:1a "For we know that if the tent which is our earthly home, is destroyed, we have a building from God." The spirit of the beings called 'humans' do not die. They are not supposed to die. They cannot rot like the body. Spirits do not die.***

Before the creation of the world and throughout the years since creation, spirits have existed to date. These include the spirits of human beings who have died since the creation of the world. All the spirits of human beings are being kept for the day of judgement. The decision of where to place the human spirits either in heaven, where God is, depends on the lives the spirits lived whilst they were attached to the earth as humans. They lived consciously given the divine rules of the earth which leads to God's heavenly kingdom. Thus judgement will be for every human being. We may not know we cannot tell why some human beings oppose this divine rule, but we believe there is a battle of the spirit in the flesh personality against other spirits who equally want them on their side at the judgement day.

> ***Romans 7:15, "I do not understand my own actions. For I do not do what I want, but I do the very thing I hate."***
>
> ***Verse 18-20 "For I know that nothing good dwells in me that is in my flesh. For I have the desire to do what is***

right, but not the ability to carry it out. For if I do not do the good, but the evil I do not want is what I keep on doing, it is no longer I who do it, but sin that dwells within me."

There is a war within the spirit of these beings called human beings with other spirit beings. These spirit beings who are against God want the human beings to equally rebel against God by either refusing to obey God's word, or make them weak to do God's will. These rebellious spirits takes their abode in the spirit of the human beings. They control the actions of those they are able to possess to rebel against God. To fight them, God has sent to humanity, power through his spirit which is Holy, to combat the demonic spirits from the spirit of human beings. God has not forced his spirit power on human beings. He makes them willing to accept his power. This Holy power of God's spirit brings humans to God's side and gives them the power to become his children by obeying God's word. This spirit was deposited into human beings from creation. They only have to make it active through obedience to God's word.

Chapter 19

MYSTERY OF THE END OF THE AGE

The mystery of the end of the world is the mystery of the fears and woes of our world today. The mystery of who will die next in a world full of deaths and pain. Having such pains as one eternal fate would be fearful. The mystery of hell's fire. What would it be like? We may not know we cannot tell but the fire service company have a clue of how hell will be because of their work. "Burning fire, do not touch my soul, Lord I pray, rescue me." We may not know we cannot tell, but we believe as Jesus prepares the mansions in heaven, hell is being prepared with fire, fire, fire. As the godly prepare with good lives to attain heaven, in the same way the ungodly prepare for hell's fire with ungodly living. Wars and rumours of wars as predicted are a clue the world is preparing to stop the clock. We may not know we cannot tell, but we believe our world is surely packing. Nature has long grown for all that humanity has done against it. They are all ready to pack. Where will be the place of people then? Heaven or hell. No more purgatory. It could be full now.

Chapter 20

THE MYSTERIOUS

It is all mysterious. Humans have not penetrated much despite what we know. It is all mystery, belonging to the one who holds humans beings and our future.

Ecclesiastes 11:7-12: 1-7

"Light is sweet and it pleases the eyes to see the sun

However many years a man live, let him enjoy them all.

But let him remember the days of darkness, for they will be many.

Everything to come is meaning less

Be happy young man while you are young.

And let your heart give you the joy in the days of your youth.

Follow the ways of your eyes and whatever your eyes see.

But know that for all these things, God will bring you to judgment.

So then banish anxiety from your heart and cast off the troubles of your body,

For youth and vigour are meaningless

Remember your creator in the days of your youth.

Before the days of trouble come and the years approach when you will say,

"I find no pleasure in them".

Before the sun and the light and the moon and the stars grows dark.

And the clouds return after the rain.

When the keepers of the house tremble and the strong men stoop.

When the grinders cease because they are few,

And those looking through the window grow dim.

When the doors to the streets are closed and the sound of grinding falls.

When men rise up at the sound of birds, but all their songs grow faint.

When men are afraid of heights and of the dangers in the streets.

When the almond tree blossoms and the grasshopper drags himself along, and the desire is no longer stirred

Then man goes to his eternal home and mourners go about the street.

Remember him before the silver cord is severed, or the golden bowl is broken:

Before the pitcher is shattered at the spring or the wheel broken at the well,

And dust returns to the ground it came from'

And the spirit returns to God who gave it."

This is also a mystery. Mystery is all over us and around us. Our life and the world are all full of mysteries.

A song writer wrote.

> ***Time changes***
> ***Times changes***
> ***Tomorrow is never known.***
> ***Only God who knows tomorrow. (Unknown writer)***

Mystery, mystery, mystery.

All are mysterious tit bits and we may not know we cannot tell, but we believe.